Mary Jokorvic

Factors Affecting Growth of SMEs in Gatundu Region North Sub-county

GRIN Verlag

Bibliografische Information der Deutschen Nationalbibliothek:

Die Deutsche Bibliothek verzeichnet diese Publikation in der Deutschen National-bibliografie; detaillierte bibliografische Daten sind im Internet über http://dnb.d-nb.de/ abrufbar.

Imprint:

Copyright © 2012 GRIN Verlag GmbH
Druck und Bindung: Books on Demand GmbH, Norderstedt Germany
ISBN: 978-3-656-63901-5

This book at GRIN:

http://www.grin.com/en/e-book/271815/factors-affecting-growth-of-smes-in-gatundu-region-north-sub-county

GRIN - Your knowledge has value

Der GRIN Verlag publiziert seit 1998 wissenschaftliche Arbeiten von Studenten, Hochschullehrern und anderen Akademikern als eBook und gedrucktes Buch. Die Verlagswebsite www.grin.com ist die ideale Plattform zur Veröffentlichung von Hausarbeiten, Abschlussarbeiten, wissenschaftlichen Aufsätzen, Dissertationen und Fachbüchern.

Factors Affecting Growth of SMEs in Gatundu Region North Sub-county

Abstract

Small and medium sized firms are the backbone of the Kenyan economy which is in the stage of progress. SMEs play a vital role in creation of employment, income generation and economic development. This qualitative study exemplifies the factors that affet the growth of SMEs within Gatundu North County in Kenya. The study adopts a critical literature review as the research strategy. The study estbalished the factors impeding growth of SMEs within Gatundu North County region in Kenya as lack of financing, poor infrastructures and central or devolved cordinating mechanisms, lack of government policy, lack of training and managerial skills, technological challenges and poor or lack of employee motivation. The study established the factors that support SMEs growth within the region as innovation in large corporations, governmental policy and partnerships with the international community. The study findings are beneficial to managers of SMEs and business students' specialicing in microfinance and SME development and general management.

Keywords: Small and medium enterprises, growth factors, Kenya.

Table of Contents

Abstract 1

Introduction 2

Literature Review... 3

Methodology 6

Findings and Discussion 7

Conclusion 11

References... 12

Introduction

About 99% of all the enterprises in the world are small or medium enterprises characterized of start up firms at the infant stage or well established SMEs. SMEs are essential in all economies especially to the developing countries characterized by major unemployment and income distribution challenges. In Kenya, SMEs are essential to the economy for which they are considered the main drivers. There are about 7.5 million SMEs in Kenya providing employment and income generating opportunities to low income sectors of the economy. The official policy framework of SMEs in Kenya is contained in the *Sessional Paper No 2 of 2005: Development of Micro and Small Enterprises for Wealth and Employment Creation for Poverty Reduction.* The policy forms the basis for enacting the SME Act which institutionalizes SME policy in Kenya (Syekei & Opijah, 2012). The contribution of the SMEs sector to the Gross Domestic Product (GDP) in Kenya increased from 13.8 percent in 1993 to about 40 percent by 2008. The sector further provides approximately 80% of the total employment and contributes about 92% of the new jobs created within the economy. The sector serves as the bedrock for industrializing the country in the future (Capital Markets Authority, 2010).

In the developing countries such as Kenya, with large informal or micro enterprise sectors, SMEs constitute the middle of the size range, hence their strategic importance. SMEs are considerably more complicated in terms of the organizational structure as opposed to microenterprises but less complicated as opposed to large corporations with layers of management and high division of labor among other characteristics. In terms of technology SMEs are intermediate between high labor intensive technologies and high capital intensive technologies providing SMEs with a special role in generation of adequate or decent employment (Palma, 2005). Due to these characteristics various constraints lower SMEs resilience to risk and prevent them from growing and attaining economies of scale. The challenges faced by SMEs in Kenya are not limited to the areas of financing investments and working capital but also include human resource development, market access and access to modern technology and information. Consequently, there are various factors that have supported SMEs growth since the 1990s (Capital Markets Authority, 2010).

In this view, this research study seeks to identify the factors affecting the growth of SMEs in the Gatundu North Sub-county. To this end, the study will establish the factors that contribute to the growth and the factors that inhibit the SMEs growth within the region. The following objectives will guide the achievement of this end: Establish the factors facilitating SMEs growth; unearth the factors inhibiting SMEs growth; and draw conclusions from the study findings. Apart from setting pace for future researchers who will be exploring SMEs growth the study may be of immediate benefit to individuals currently managing SMEs.

Literature Review

This chapter presents a review of existing literature on the factors inhibiting and facilitating the growth of SMEs. According to Capital Markets Authority (CMU) (2010), Kenyan SMEs lack access to financing though most SMEs tend to be located in urban and peri-urban areas and are usually registered. SMEs usually rely on the banking sector and other financial intermediaries for financial instruments for financing working capital and providing short-term liquidity management. The financial instruments are not always forthcoming in the required amounts as banks evaluate SMEs on the basis of a checklist made of audited financial statement, project proposals, financial projection, monitoring costs, credit or default risk and enforcement costs. Carrier (1999) argues that SMEs are considered a high risk activity that generates transaction costs and low returns on investment by many financial providers. Where provided, the financial products fail to meet the expectations of SMEs thus frustrating the SMEs efforts of achieving the set business efforts. Carrier (1999) argues that improving access to finance small and medium enterprises is crucial in fostering entreprenuership, competition, innovation and growth in Kenya.

Longenecker et al. (2006) attributes the failure of SMEs to poor or lack of planning, improper financing and poor management. This challenge is compounded by lack of education or vocational training in most of the SMEs managers. Lack of training creates possibilities of simple management mistakes which considerably lead to enterprise failure (Bowen, Morara & Mureithi, 2009). Managerial competencies are very significant to the continued existence and enlargement of new SMEs. Lack of education and training concentrates management aptitude in new firms leading to low level entrepreneurial formation and high collapse rates of new business enterprises (Olawale, 2010). Management at the SME level is characterized by development of own management approaches which are based on intuition and opportunistic rather than analytical and strategic. This creates problems especially in occasions which demand complex decisions. Poor managerial ability further results in poor change management and consequent failure. Competition is a major challenge to SMEs as most small enterprises congregate in dense markets and overcrowded cities. Competition as a challenge is further compounded by lack of market information and innovation leading to duplication of already existing businesses. SMEs have also to contend with globalization which presents challenges such as increased competition and opportunities

(Bowen, Morara & Mureithi, 2009). Lack of or poor employee motivation affects employee performance resulting in low productivity. Due to low motivation levels, employees divert their energy into features not related to an organization's work such as individual conversation, internet surfing and captivating longer lunches which cost SMEs time and money. William (2012) argues that concentrated efficiency is harmful to an organization's recital and future achievement or growth.

The sector further lacks central coordinating mechanisms and devolved coordinating and implementation mechanism leading to failures since the sector requires better support systems either from the government or collective action by the SMEs themselves than those required by larger firms. Poor infrastructures especially pose a major challenge to SMEs in Kenya. The provision of better infrastructure has lagged behind over the years. Infrastructural challenges such as poor roads and inadequate electricity supply still derail development initiatives and the informal sector at large in spite of government after government promising infrastructural developments.

Technological changes pose a great threat to small businesses. Since the mid-1990s there has been a growing concern about the impact of technological change on micro and small business. Small businesses are especially disadvantaged by technological changes due to the unfamiliarity with new technologies. This challenge is experienced by even the well positioned SMEs which are located in the urban and peri-urban areas. SMEs are often unaware of technological changes and where aware the technology is unavailable or unaffordable. Muteti (2005) argues that in most developing countries, inclusive of Kenya; experience the challenge of connecting indigenous small enterprises with foreign investors and speeding up technological upgrading. The digital divide between the rural and urban Kenya is too wide as most rural areas lack power supply and internet connectivity. This creates challenges in accessing information or information networks that are core in enterprise development. This further creates challenges in accessing sufficient market information despite the availability of trade-related information and the possibility of accessing national and international data. Muteti (2005) argues that most small enterprises heavily rely on private or physical contacts for market related information due to inabilities to interpret statistical data. Government policy significantly impacts technology decisions at the enterprise level. The structural adjustment programs (SAPs) implemented in many African countries aim at removing heavy policy distortions which are detrimental to private sector growth. However, SAPs severely affect vulnerable groups in the short run. According to Wanjohi and Mugure (2008) business environment is a key factor that affects the growth of

SMEs. Unpredictable government policies coupled by grand corruption and high taxation rates greatly threaten the sustainability of SMEs and the Kenyan economy in general.

Consequently, various factors have contributed towards the growth of SMEs within Kenya. The government for example has realized the role of SMEs in the economy and has in the past few years improved its efforts in SME development. The key organs of the government such as parliament and related policymaking institutions such as local authorities has set institutional frameworks facilitating easier licensing and provided appropriate incentives to facilitate performance. The Kenya Local Government Reform Program (KLGRP) enacted in 1999 has particularly effective in reducing poverty and employment and spurring the economy to higher rates of growth. The KLGRP was specifically structured to eliminate unnecessary regulatory barriers and the reduction of costs of doing business. Through the reform the government initiated the Single Business Permit (SBP) and the Local Transfer Fund (LATF) as a response to business licensing problems experienced by SMEs. The government has further created programs for funding budding entrepreneurs through programs such as The Youth Fund aimed at providing loans to groups of youth entrepreneurs, the Kenya Women Trust Fund and the CDF kitty aimed at supporting constituency level, grass-root development projects. The CDF kitty has promoted the development and growth of SMEs in rural areas through improvement of supporting infrastructures (Wanjohi & Mugure, 2008).

Innovations in large corporations trickle down to the Middle and Small Enterprises (MSE) sector resulting in increased efficiency, productivity and growth in SMEs. This is especially evident in the case of mobile money transfer services offered by the various telecommunications companies in the country such as Safaricom, Airtel, Orange and Yu. Safaricom has especially led the other corporation in introducing innovative services such as M-pesa and recently M-shwari. These innovations have provided SMEs with alternative means of transacting as customers can pay for services through M-pesa. SMEs can also obtain fast loans from mobile money lending services such as M-shwari. These means of transaction have improved the security of transactions. Establishment of a connection between banking services and mobile banking services through services such as M-kesho has made it easier to access funds and further improved security by reducing the physical transportation of funds.

The international community through various initiatives has supported the growth of the SME sub-sector. Certain international organizations have been in the fore line in facilitating networks and partnerships in the SME sector. For example, UNIDO has played a key role in assisting business networks from various SMEs sectors and providing direct assistance to professional organizations in Africa. In order to facilitate access to funding by networking SMEs, international development partners such as UNIDO partner with local banks and credit associations facilitating development of new schemes providing mutual guarantee funds for the SMEs sector. Such schemes provide suitable conditions for projects through mobilization of multi-stakeholder working groups, including local government, private sector representatives and civil society organizations. This results into reinforced managerial and technical competencies and better coordination of future joint ventures in the SMEs sector (UNIDO, 2002).

Methodology

As argued by Trochim (2000), the research methodology details the activities/procedures that were carried out by the researcher in the process of seeking to provide answers(s) to the prevailing research question(s). On the same note, the research methodology also explains how the research progress was measured as well as the expected results after the research study. As such, this section presents the methods that were deemed appropriate and thus applied in the process of establishing the challenges and the factors that facilitate growth of SMEs in Kenya.

Bryman (2001) notes that a researcher can apply either qualitative or quantitative data analysis method or a mixed method design which combines the utility of both. For the purposes of this study, a qualitative research design was considered as the most effective analysis method to provide interpretations and explanations of the challenges faced by SMEs and the factors that facilitate growth of SMEs within Kenya. This study can be considered as illustrative study since the focal point is on the discovery of success factors and challenge factors of Kenyan SMEs.

The process of data collection in a research study is highly significant as it enables the researcher to seek answers to the prevailing research questions through collecting information from the right sources (Bryman, 2001). In this view, a researcher can utilize; primary data, secondary data, or a combination of both in the process of answering the research questions. In the process of establishing the challenges and the factors that facilitate the growth of SMEs in Kenya, secondary data collection method was utilized whereby data was collected from journals, books, periodicals, documentaries, newspapers, and web articles among other materials that were deemed to have appropriate information on SMEs, the challenges faced by SMEs and the growth factors for SMEs.

Findings and Discussion

Soini and Veseli (2011) argue that most SMEs in the developing world, such as Kenya and Kosovo experience lack of access to credit as the main obstacle. In their study among SMEs in Kosovo, the authors established that only a minimal percentage (10%) of SMEs is financed through credit while the major percentage (85%) are established from the entrepreneur's own efforts. This is emphasized by the findings of Bowen, Morara and Mureithi (2009), among entrepreneurs in Nairobi, whereby most of the entrepreneurs within the region acknowledged that most SMEs mainly rely on own savings and reinvested profits to finance the businesses. According to a study by Ahmad et al. (2012), one of the extraneous factors affecting SMEs in Pakistan is lack of finances. The authors argue that, SMEs in developing countries face important barriers to economics. Though many sectors in the developing world experience financial restraints, SMEs is mostly controlled by gaps in the physical structure such as high administrative costs, high swear material and lack of information inside economic intermediaries. As such, facilitating easier access to financing for SMEs creates better fiscal circumstances in the developing world by promoting novelty, macro-economic softness and GDP growth (Ahmed et al., 2012). Soini and Veseli (2011) argue that there is a need to strengthen risk management instruments that increase the willingness of lending institutions such as banks to lend to SMEs. According to CMA (2010), the smaller the enterprise the less likelihood of its management understands the need for financial management and the poorer the understanding of financial management. The distance from major cities/urban centers is negatively related to the level of awareness of financial instruments. SMEs situated farther away from cities or urban centers are less aware of available financial instruments. This makes them vulnerable to revenue and cost shocks limiting the capability to expand beyond certain limits. The turnover of a majority of the SMEs in Kenya is estimated at a mere Kshs. 5 million a year. Poor returns, lack of sound financial records and lack of collateral make most SMEs not creditworthy (CMA, 2010). The lack of access to finance by SMEs further creates a need to develop and strengthen micro-finance institutions that have the potential to lend to rural entrepreneurs. This transforms the existing non-profit foundations into more suitable, for profit financial intermediaries thus raising awareness of the potential roles of small entrepreneurs in the mainstream economic activities. In Kenya micro-finance institutions have gained shape thus creating an alternative source of credit and finances for small scale entrepreneurs.

Lack of management competencies plaque most SMEs in the developing world. Ahmed at al. (2012) established lack of management competencies as one of the factors hindering success in Pakistan SMEs. Soini and Veseli (2011) also established entrepreneurial influences such as managerial knowledge as a major factor among SMEs in Kosovo. Soini and Veselli (2011) argue that SMEs owners have considerable personal influence over firm strategies, tactics and operations engage in decision process across the firm. Most SMEs adopts flat and informal organizational structures with decision making centralized around the owner. The entrepreneur's personality and behavior are causal factors for or against growth oriented achievement. Since power decisions in SMEs are centralized at the level of owner-manager, the personality, skills, responsibilities, attitude and behavior have a decisive influence on business strategy (Levy & Powell, 2005). Ahmed et al. (2012) posit management competencies as a set of facts, skills, behaviors and approaches that contribute to individual usefulness. Managerial competencies are significant to the continued existence and enlargement of new and existing SMEs. Most SMEs lack obvious tactics for prospect growth, production procedures, marketing and fiscal behaviors. Due to the holdup of the decision making method, where decisions are made by a single individual, SMEs are deprived association and exposed to poor employment, weak scheming and directing, poor money management and especially lack of methodological account keeping. The situation is compounded by lack of general official training in the SMEs sector. Training is central to knowledge based industries and economic growth. Well accomplished and malleable personnel are important to economic progress. Training results in economic benefits for SMEs through the human capital generated from training. On the same note, training is a crucial factor for the productivity and quality of decisions as it influences effectiveness, efficiency and motivation of the employees in SMEs (Ahmed et al., 2012). Bowen, Morara and Mureithi (2009) posit education as one of the factors that impact positively on growth of firms. As such, the entrepreneurs with large stocks of human capital, in terms of education and vocational training are better positioned in adapting their enterprises to the constantly changing business environment.

Access to public corporeal infrastructure comprise of water, electricity, serviceable roads, telecommunications, electronic media and postal services. These services are crucial for business startups, development and growth. Limited access to infrastructure services therefore constraints SME growth and survival by limiting operations and restricting access to markets and raw materials (Ahmed et al, 2012). Public infrastructure affects the number of firms opening in metropolitan and rural areas showing that public capital stock positively affects employment growth through business startups and expansion. This is emphasized by Soini and Veseli (2011) who argue that business accessibility is a crucial factor for growth.

Public infrastructure such as serviceable roads and telecommunications networks improve the accessibility of SMEs in the current and future consumer base. The business location has an implication on the labor and transport costs, proximity to suppliers and work disruption due to infrastructural challenges such as power outage and poor road networks. Tustin (2001), emphasize that geographic location has implications on access to markets and other resources such as finance, skilled labour, subcontractors, infrastructure, distribution and transportation logistics among other facilities. Proper infrastructure facilitated efficient coordination of business activities thus linking consumers with small and medium service providers in essence leading to growth and development of both the formal and informal SME sub-sectors. In Kenya, the government through the Kenya Power Company is making an initiative to electrify the rural areas through the rural electrification initiative aimed at empowering rural areas business through electricity. In spite of the efforts, a study by Bowen, Morara and Mureithi (2009) established that most SMEs within Nairobi face the challenge of constant power outage which impairs operations thus inhibiting growth.

Competition threatens a firm's survival but is also the main factor for economic growth as it derives firms to improve productivity therefore driving growth (Soini & Vaseli, 2011). Duplication of services and products coupled with globalization compounds the competition as entrepreneurs have to seek for innovative measures to counter the competition for enterprise survival. Entrepreneurs within Nairobi highlighted good customer service followed by discount offers, use of price as a competitive edge by selling cheaply, credit facilities, offering quality goods and services and after sale services such as free training as some of the competitive measures adopted by SMEs. Use of price as a competitive measure result into lower profits though it translates into higher sale volumes (Bowen, Morara & Mureithi, 2010). Analysing competitor activities and developing counter competition intelligence and actions is crucial for SME survival. Philips (2006) argues that SMEs for survival must compete based on their strengths and specialization focused on cost leadership and differentiation. This creates the need for tighter controls on operational costs; efficient production and providing products that capture the market, have high service levels, and adopt a unique distribution and non-standard terms of business. SMEs must further focus on particular market segments and adopt continued improvement in quality, cost, lead times and customer service and flexibility.

Technologies provide SMEs with opportunities and challenges. Technology creates an opportunity for SMEs to transform to knowledge driven firms in a business environment where knowledge and information are essential and a key factor in production and where ideas, processes, knowledge and information are a growing share of trade (Pollard, 2006). SMEs require effective information systems to support and deliver information to different users. Such systems must include decision support systems to support management decisions and provide information for supporting organizational processes. Technological changes pose a threat to small business due to the high occurrence rates. SMEs are disadvantaged by the rapidly changing technologies due to lack of technical know how of operating new technologies and the lack of finances to upgrade to newer and more efficient technologies. These factors coupled with poor telecommunications infrastructure hinder SMEs from accessing information networks that are core in enterprise development (Muteti, 2005).

Partnerships between the public and the private sector or between firms in the private sector boost SMEs growth as indicated by innovations in the private sector trickling down to the SME sub sector. Ahmed et al. (2012) argue that cooperation between the public and the private sector is the most competent and efficient apparatus. Such cooperation creates community and confidential company aptitude of co-responsibility and co-ownership thus endorsing small enterprises. This results in vitality, right of entry, easier financing and access to support services to SMEs. This is achievable through SME networks designed to assist SMEs gain access to commercial markets, improve information sharing or developing structures to allow companies to share human resources in state affairs. Such networks assist SMEs agreement with impact of disasters in conditions of the preserves of employment, productivity and market split by pooling resources together (Ahmed et al., 2012). In Kenya, partnerships between large corporations such as Safaricom and Equity Bank has benefited SMEs by easing access to money and offering alternative means of transacting. Cooperation between private banks and micro-financial institutions and government agencies has improved and eased access to funding for SMEs. However, there is still need for increased governmental involvement through policy development activities aimed at further easing access to credit for SMEs and creating an attractive business environment in order to boost the growth and performance of the SME sub sector by eliminating beuriacracy, combatting inflation, and eliminating high taxation on the sector (Wanjohi & Mugure, 2008).

The international community through development intiatives enhances the growth of SMEs. Memba, Gakure and Karanja (2012) argue that business organizations, voluntary organizations and other non-governmental organizations have set up programs to enhace the factors that influence development of SME especially in relation to enterprise growth and development. The services offered by organizations from the international community vary and range from the provision of financial assistance, training and extension services, preconstructed commercial shades and assisting in marketing products. International organizations further enhance the growth of SMEs by promoting the establishment of crucial networks between the public and the private sector, thus improving the access to funding and providing SMEs with technical assistance and training or linking SMEs with international markets for products (Ahmed et al., 2012). To this end, international organizations partner with local and international banks and other international development partners or credit associations to create schemes aimed at empowering the SME sub sector.

Conclusion

It is evident that SMEs face multifarious factors which inhibit their growth and development. Consequently various factors have contributed to the growth of SMEs within Kenya. The government needs to be actively involved in order to boost the SMEs growth through policy development, easing access to funding and developing supporting infrastructures such as roads, electricity and telecommunications networks. The banking sector plays an important role in providing financial support for SMEs. However, there is a need for increased innovation in development of financial products befitting the SMEs sector. Such products should be developed in a manner improves credit accessibility by removing impositions placed by lending institutions on SMEs and enhancing the ability of SMEs to repay credit facilities. Public and private institutions should partner and provide technological support to SMEs thus enhancing the ability of SMEs to cope with technological changes. This can be done as community development initiatives or creating technology support centers from which SMEs can outsource technological services. The government should work towards reducing the digital divide between the rural and urban areas through electrification projects in order to enhance the establishment and growth of SMEs in rural regions such as a Gatundu North County. The government and individual entrepreneurs must make an initiative to gain management skills in order to enhance proper management of SMEs. Through government initiative the number of institutions offering tertiary education in the country has increased. SMEs must therefore make initiatives to provide their managers with basic management skills for growth. SMEs must also come up with competitive strategies in order to survive local and global competition and thus enhance their survival. This can be achieved through cost differentiation, organizational positioning and provision of innovative products. Large corporations have to provide support for the SME sub-sector through innovations aimed at improving the means of doing business in Kenya and enhance technology

12

attainment, diffusion and continually engage inter-firm manufacture relations and institutional support with SMEs.

References

Ahmed, M., Ahmad, E., Kahut, M.B.H, & Murtaza, G. (2012). New determination of factors affecting the growth of small and medium enterprises in Pakistan. *Interdisciplinary Journal of Contemporary Research in Business, 4*(6), 513-530.

Bowen, M., Morara, M., & Mureithi, S. (2009). Management of business challenges among small and micro enterprises in Nairobi, Kenya. *KCA Journal of Business Management, 2*(1), 16-31.

Bryman, A. (2001). *Social research methods.* New York: Oxford University Press.

Capital Markets Authority, (2010). Capital raising opportunities for SMEs: The development of micro-cap securities markets in Kenya. Nairobi: Capital Markets Authority.

Carrier, C., (1999), "The Training and Development Needs of Owner-manager of Small Businesses with Export Potential", *Journal of Small Business Management*, July, PP. 30- 41.

King, K. and McGrath, S. (2002). Globalization, Enterprise and Knowledge. Symposium, Oxford.

Levy, M., Powell, P. (2005) strategies for growth in SMEs: The Role of Information and Information Systems.

Longenecker, J. G., Petty, C. W., Moore, J. W. and Palich, L. E. (2006). Small Business Management, An entrepreneurial emphasis. London: Thomson South Western.

Memba, S.F., Gakure, W.R., & Karanja, K. (2012). Venture capital (VC): Its impact on growth of small and medium enterprises in Kenya. *International Journal of Business and Social Science, 3* (6), 32-38.

Muteti, J. (2005). SME Lecture Notes. Nairobi: The Catholic University of Eastern Africa (CUEA).

Olawale, F. (2010). Obstacles to the growth of new SMEs in South Africa: A principal componentanalysis approach. *African Journal of Business Management Vol. 4(5), pp. 729-738, May 2010* , 731.

Palma, G. (2005) "Four Sources of De-industrialization and a New Concept of the 'Dutch Disease'" in JoseAntonio Ocampo (editor) Beyond Reform: Structural Dynamics and Macroeconomic Vulnerability. Stanford, Calif.: Stanford University Press.

Philip, W.A. (2006) Strategic Entrepreneurship 4th Edition.

Pollard, D. (2006): Promoting Learning Transfer. *Developing SME Marketing Knowledge in the Dnipropetrovsk Oblast*, Ukraine.

Soini, E., & Veseli, L. (2011). Factors influencing SMEs growth in Kosovo. Turku University of Applied Sciences, Turku, Finland.

Syekei, J., & Opijah, D. (2012). Kenya's vision 20130: Creating more dinner space for SMEs on the IP table. Retrieved 20 March 2013, http://www.coulsonharney.com/News-Blog/Blog/Creating-more-dinner-space-for-SMEs

Trochim, W. (2000). *The Research Methods Knowledge Base*, 2nd Edition. Atomic Dog Publishing, Cincinnati: OH.

Tustin, D.B. (2001).Capitalism & democracy in the 21st Century: From the Managed to the entrepreneurial economy. *Journal of Evolutionary Economics*, 10, 17-34.

United Nation Industrial Development organization (UNIDO) (2002). Stimulating SME environment. Retrieved March 20 2013 from www.unido.org.

Wanjohi, A.M. and Mugure, A. (2008). Factors affecting the growth of MSEs in rural areas of Kenya: A case of ICT firms in Kiserian Township, Kajiado District of Kenya.

Williams, S. (2012). How Does Employee Motivation Impact Organizational Performance? Retrieved from eHOW Money: www.ehow.com › Business